T0078407

THE FIRE COULDN'T BURN ME

DR. MELINDA WATTS

ANGELA SINKFIELD-GRAY – EDITOR

WESTBOW
PRESS®
A DIVISION OF THOMAS NELSON
& ZONDERVAN

WestBow Press books may be ordered through booksellers or by contacting:

WestBow Press
A Division of Thomas Nelson & Zondervan
1663 Liberty Drive
Bloomington, IN 47403
www.westbowpress.com
844-714-3454

ISBN: 978-1-6642-6795-4 (sc)
ISBN: 978-1-6642-6796-1 (e)

Print information available on the last page.

WestBow Press rev. date: 07/18/2022

DEDICATION

I dedicated this book to my husband, Ronald Watts, for his commitment to supporting me during the process of writing this book. He patiently sacrificed his time to allow me the space to write. I love and appreciate your sacrifice. I pray that the Lord will give back to you a one hundredfold blessing my rib. I pray for the blessing of the Lord upon our union and that we will continue to grow together in the things of God and use the gifts and talents that he has bestowed upon us to bless the world. Again, thank you. Love your wife.

I also dedicated this book to the memories of my mother, Addie Mae Walker and my father, Avery Bryant. I will always be forever grateful for the legacy they left me. My Father who encouraged me to pursue education because he was unable to do so. My mother who taught me that it doesn't matter how you start; it matters how you finish. She also gave me her tenacity despite the adversities, never quit. I am now fulfilling their legacy.

I also dedicated this book to my children, Jarod and Phaedra Jones. I appreciate your love and support. You both have made me proud to be your mother. It is because of you and my future grandchildren that I pursue greatness. My desire is to leave a legacy for both of you and future generations. Psalms 71: 18 Now also when I am old and gray, O God forsake me not; until I have shewed thy strength unto this generation, and that power to everyone that is to come. This is my prayer daily. I pray I inspire you to be the best you can be and follow your dreams.

I am grateful for the influence of Author Lorieen Henry, my confidant, prayer warrior and friend. My intercessor Aukeyshia Tate. I can say so much about these ladies. They held my arms up when I wanted to wave the white flag. Elder Lorieen Henry, I thank you for being my biggest cheerleader. The words of encouragement you gave me inspired me to finish this book. The vase you gave me before you left the island of Oahu, which you used on your first book signing, is ready for use. It has such sentimental value. My prayer warrior Aukeyshia you were obedient to the Lord to speak this word to me.

"I see you writing books, "and now I am releasing my first book. Thank you for your steadfast prayers. I found you to be a force to be reckoned with. So many times, you would send me messages that were so on point. Thank you for your love, prayer, support and steadfastness in the Lord and your gift to speak life to me in so many ways. I pray that the Lord will richly bless both of you.

I would like to thank my friend, my sister in Christ, Dr. Angela Sinkfield - Gray for her insight, confidence, and support in assisting me with publishing my writing. I praise God for your expertise. I am forever grateful.

I've learned in life that there is a hero inside everyone. I thank God, my Father, for the greater inside of me that gave me the courage to press even when I wanted to quit. My hero is Jesus Christ, my Rock and because of him, I survived and became more than a conqueror. I can now say with power and demonstration, the fire could not burn me.

PREFACE

We all have a beginning. That beginning has been predestined by the Lord. We have the right to choose this day who we will serve. We were created to glorify God in everything. That which we go through is for purpose. Our testimony is the answer to someone else's deliverance. The Holy Spirit is there to gently lead and guide us if we allow him permission into our hearts. The Lord desires none to perish. That is the reason he came to this earth. We all have a story to tell. The outcome of our story depends on our obedience to the Will of God for our lives. He said I stand at the door and I knock. Unless we as individuals open up our hearts and allow him to come in and sup with us, the deliverance cannot take place. The beginning of man's life can be challenging. It is not how we start but how we finish. The Lord desires to make the crooked places straight. I am grateful for the eye-opening experience that changed my life drastically. We must believe what the word of God says about our life. Once we recognize we have an adversary and his job is to steal, kill and destroy then our deliverance can take place. The key is recognizing who the real enemy is and then allow Jesus, who is our ransom to rescue us from our situations. The fire of rejection, lies, and defeat can be conquered when we make the exchange and let God's consuming fire burn away the pain of our past and future hurts, disappointments and defeats. Always remember God wastes no pain. He wants to turn our ashes into beauty if we allow him to. Just know the fire that he uses is meant to redefine, realign, and refine us.

CONTENTS

CHAPTER 1
THE BEGINNING

D.C. General Hospital

E verything starts with a beginning. The beginning is a time or space at which something starts. ***Genesis 1:1-2 KJV states "In the beginning, God created heavens and the earth. 2. Now the earth was formless and empty, darkness was over the surface of the deep, and the Spirit of God was hovering over the waters. God said let there be light, and there was light."***

In the beginning, God created me, Melinda Walker -Watts; my life was without form, and void; I was born at District of Columbia General Hospital on August 26,1965, at 10:50 pm and darkness was upon me.

It is not what happens to you in life; it matters how you deal with it. I have seen individuals go through far worse situations than I have and to this day, it is affecting their lives. The book, The Scarlet Letter reminds me of my mother's pain because she got pregnant with me while being married and it affected us greatly. The stereotyping was hurtful and degrading for her as well as me. I was ashamed and made to feel like I was a mistake and unloved. I know now it was in the plan of God. He can make all things new. I am grateful that the path God chose for me did not define my destiny or my identity. One thing about life is that we can choose our friends, but we cannot choose our family. It wasn't always pleasant, but we survived, and it made us stronger. Although we endured ridicule and persecution, we became overcomers. ***Jeremiah 29:11 NIV says, "For I know the plans I have for you declares the Lord, plans to prosper you and not to harm you plans to give you hope and a future."***

When I was yet in my mother's womb, he ordained me. ***Jeremiah 1:5 NIV "Before I formed you in the womb I knew you, before you were born, I set you apart; I appointed you as a prophet to the nations."***

I was born with purpose and destiny inside me, and I didn't even know it yet.

My birth certificate said I was born to Addie Mae and Garland Walker but as time went on, my identity was revealed. I was told lies about my birth. My aunt told me that my mother went into premature labor with me because she was avoiding danger for me as well as for herself.

In the beginning, the devil's plot was to destroy my life. I can identify with Jesus how Satan used Herod the King to plot to destroy him. However, the angel of the Lord appeared to Joseph and warned him to go in another direction. My aunt and many others were angels for me and my mother. The story goes when my mother laid eyes on me, she fainted.

As an intervention, my aunt had to intervene. My mother knew instantly I was not Garland's daughter. My features were totally different. I was dark-skinned, and Garland was a light-skinned man. My mother's blood pressure went up and she fainted when she saw me. I found out that my mother was discharged from the hospital, but I remained a little longer. When I was discharged, my aunt took me home because she knew she couldn't allow me to go home with her brother-in-law for fear of the outcome.

My birthday has always been exciting to me. I always felt special on my birthday. I shared the same day with my mother's aunt and grandmother's sister; her name was Aunt Thelma.

Thelma

My Aunt Thelma made sure my birthday was celebrated. She was one of the many angels in the form of a human. She made sure I received twenty dollars every birthday. That was our little secret. I also believe my grandmother had a lot to do with that as well.

In my early years, I was impacted by angels in the form of human beings that helped form my destiny. My beginning was preordained by God. I know that individuals were placed in my life to equip me for my life's journey. I experienced love from so many family members from both sides of my parents' family. In those rough moments, the angels appeared to ensure I received the necessities like love and support that I really needed. It always amazed me how their timing was on point. I always had a vivid imagination and always sought to see the good in everything I went through early in my childhood. I was often made fun of because I talked to myself and had imaginary friends; this encouraged me to deal with certain traumatic situations in my life. I would say things like I am going to be a secretary and have two children and my name will be Mrs. Jones and I am going to live far away. I have always been a very vivid dreamer. I would dream things and they would happen just as I dreamt it. We often hear people say that's déjà vu. The definition of deja vu is a feeling of having already experienced the present situation.

At an early age I would see things and I would speak things into existence and it would happen. I know now that it is the gift of prophecy that I was born with. A lot of times I would be afraid of the things I saw and I was afraid to share it with my mother and others so I kept it to myself. I learned how to suppress this gift because I was talked about.. I found strength and humor in superheroes and fairy tales. I believed that if you could imagine, it would happen. In those early years, I did not know Christ. However, he knew me, and he had his hand in my life. I would say things and speak about what I wanted to happen in my life. I ultimately saw these things come to pass in my life.

My beginning was nothing I would have chosen for my life; however, it was what the Lord allowed. I understand the scripture now when it says don't despise the day of small beginnings. The Lord uses small beginning to develop great leaders. My beginning was a place of humility. My beginning would be one of those, "Leave it to Beaver," family lives. A mother and father under the same roof, a house with a white picket fence and financial stability. I watched my mother raise five children on her own. We lived in a community where families helped one another. Our family did not have much but we survived the worse of time. As I ponder over my life's journey, I see the word of God being fulfilled in my life.

In every individual's life, there is a beginning. Ecclesiastes says it well. There is a time to be born and a time to die. Its' our birthing season. Our development depends on how we view our life. I have seen people still struggling with how their life started "their beginning." I discovered if left unresolved a bad beginning can hinder how you handle life. As I share parts of my life with the world, I want my beginning to testify that although life served me lemons; I made lemonade with the guidance of the Holy Spirit. The Lord can change your story for his glory. It doesn't matter if you were born in marriage, out of wedlock or due to infidelity, etc. It does not determine your life's outcome.

I have seen dysfunction in two-parent homes as well as single-parent homes. However, if you allow people to stereotype your circumstances and categorize you, it hinders your growth, which affects you in the long run.

I have also witnessed the emotional and mental anguish that comes with the repercussion of life's choices of family trauma caused by loved ones and left unresolved. It affects people's emotional development, and results in them not being able to cope with life situations. Often the enemy's desire for us as God's chosen people is to stay stuck in the past, not forgiving our ancestors, resulting in generational curses. The curses are then passed on to the next generation.

I am grateful for my encounter with Christ. He exposed my nakedness, took my formless beginning, and shaped it into a testimony. It's not how your life starts; it's how you finish. ***(Phil. 1:6 NIV) "He who began a good work in you will carry it on till completion...."*** We must speak life over ourselves and trust the process.

Grandma you will always be in my heart

Let me Fast forward. I would like to journey into my adolescent years. I loved the TV show "The Beverly Hillbillies". It reflected the next move in our family's life. In my mind, it took us out of a place of hardship to a place of a new beginning and healthier structure. When we moved to Takoma Park, Maryland, with our grandmother and uncles, my journey took a turn for the better for me. My grandmother Hattie Bernice Patterson was my everything. She was the best grandmother ever to me.

She was an outstanding cook. She could make something out of nothing. Her personality was humorous, witty, and feisty. My grandmother was my biggest cheerleader. I felt comfortable talking to her about anything. I learned so much from her and my uncles during our stay there. In addition, we had good times and our bad times as all families. I prefer to focus on the good times and learn what to do and what not to do from the bad times.

Mom + Dad

Our house was a community home. It was never a dull moment there. Our grandfather was a carpenter, and I was told he helped build the house we once resided in. I vaguely remember my grandfather. I heard stories of my grandparent's union. I was told they were inseparable. As I learned more about them, they had their ups and downs; however, they stayed together until death parted them from one another.

Our family home held so many positive memories for me. I looked forward to the summers when all the first cousins would come and stay for the whole summer. Our uncles played a major role in making sure we had fun family trips and gatherings like going to Sandy Point Beach, cooking out at Spring Park, cooking out in the back yard, and going across the yard to Uncle Scooby's house to play pool and other games, it was the highlight of my day. I loved watching my mother. aunts, and uncles interact. They loved dancing and partying. We would have a dance contest and I would win every time, my mother and her siblings came together. We, as children, were not allowed to be around the grown folks. However, I would sneak around the house or go upstairs and peek out the window so I could learn some of the latest dance moves. As always, I was curious George, so in the aftermath of our adult family gatherings, my cousin and I would call ourselves cleaning up the backyard emptying beer cans and sweeping cigarette butts up all the while sampling them as well.

Uncle Scoobie

My Uncle Scoobie. Wow! I can say so much about this amazing man. He is the backbone of the family. We never lacked anything if he knew about it.

He ensured that we had everything we needed and most of what we wanted. I thought he was the coolest person ever. During the era when I was growing up, there was a movie called, "Superfly" and to me, he was a super person to our family. He loved his family unconditionally. He made sure we inherited our family traditions. His untimely death left a large whole in our family's heart.

Our family traditions were family time, cooking, traveling and bonding; this was very important. Our grandmother and uncles made sure we learned these attributes. The highlights of the Patterson family gatherings were eating dinner together and holiday fellowship.

I am not sure if people even eat four meals a day now. We had breakfast, lunch, dinner and supper. Our daily routine was to eat together as a family. Each day, one of the Patterson crew had to stand between Popular Avenue and Spring Avenue and yell supper time which was at six' o'clock in the evening. We could not be late. If we were late, we did not eat. We had to pass grand mom's inspections in which she made sure we washed our hands before we sat at the table. We couldn't talk at the table. If we did, we had more food added to our plates. After finishing our meals, we had to ask to be dismissed from the dinner table. The Holidays were very special, Especially Thanksgiving; Uncle Scooby taught us how to peel potatoes and cut collards. I remember he took the knife and told me don't be scared. It's hard to cut your thumb. He was so patient with me. I was scared to use a knife, lol. Cooking was the highlight of the Patterson family.

The only thing I hated about Thanksgiving was those wild turkeys and coons my grandmother would have in those black trash bags. They were frightening to look at. It was the preparations I didn't like. Those animals were ugly and scary-looking before they were cleaned. I would have nightmares about them chasing me.

My favorite holiday has always been Christmas. Our family was always excited about the Christmas shows that came on television, you know like Frosty the Snowman, Charlie Brown's Christmas, Rudolph the Red Nose Reindeer etc... Our grandmother made sure the house was decorated beautifully and smelled good. I loved the story she told me about the big black Santa Claus that came every year.

I will always believe in the joy of Christmas. I am so blessed that my ancestors did not rob me as a child of the gift of expecting and wishing and believing that if you ask for special things you can receive it based on your obedience. The scripture is true as well *Matthew 7:7 NIV "Ask and it will be given to you; seek and you will find; knock and the door will be opened to you.* The mystery of Christmas is a choice. I am glad I know the real meaning of it.

For me, it is an opportunity to share Christ by giving. In life, I've learned to see the beauty in all things. *Philippians 4:8 KJV... if there be any virtue, if there be any praise, think on these things.* The praise I have is for the family love we shared during this time of the year. It was my happy place.

I would tell my grandmother my wishes and it never failed; on Christmas morning, I would have exactly what I asked for. She would tell me that the big black Santa Claus had come. That's the way she got me to be good. I was known for being a tattletale. My grandmother threatened me that the big black Santa Claus would not bring me any good presents if I was disobedient. She always encouraged me to be the best person I could be and make a difference in my life. Her words of wisdom were to finish school and wait to have children. My grandmother, her sisters and I had a unique bond.

I never met my Aunt Willie Mae and Uncle Jeff until years later in my life

The Posy Sisters

My Aunt Pudding, Aunt Thelma, Hattie B, my girl and Aunt Earline made sure my Christmas was extra special. I looked forward to that day because they would always call my grandmother and say did my baby get her Christmas wish and then they would laugh about the big black Santa Claus. I was so naïve I would say to my grandmom don't make fun of Santa Claus, or he won't bring you anything next year. She then would tell me to stay out of grown people's conversations.

My Aunt Thelma would then say, "send my baby around here to get her present". My gift would be her famous bread pudding and twenty dollars. In addition, I became a personal runner; let me explain. My grandmother had a drinking problem which resulted in her having a stroke years ago. The stroke confined her to a wheelchair. A few of her sisters were her enablers and I was the accomplice to the crime. I was taught to obey my elders and not ask many questions.

Now that I am older, I understand I was not helping my grandmother but aiding her addictions. I would go pick up this brown-bag not knowing it had her (CC) Canadian Club in it.

My great aunts loved my biological father, so I received special treatment because of that. At that time, I did not know he was my father. My grandmother's bond with her sisters was priceless. They talked every day for hours, and I can remember them falling asleep on each other on the phone. My Aunt Pudding was the great aunt that taught me about the history of the family in the south. She would always tease me about my eyes and big smile. I really enjoyed going to her house during the summer, especially when her daughter Minnie Lee would come and visit with her children from South Carolina.

Our family's lineage was very blessed, and we had a lot of fun. It was there I learned about my mother's oldest brother Clarence Posey. I knew him as Uncle Bobby. He looked just like my grandmother. He had a different father from my mother and her siblings. I was told that my great-grandmother raised him. I had the opportunity to spend time with him and his family. I really admired him because he and I shared similar stories. He had a different father and so did I.

As I spent time with him, it gave me hope to believe that you can achieve anything if you put your mind and heart into it. Although he was separated from my grandmother, he still thrived and accomplished great things in his life. He inspired me to seek better for my life.

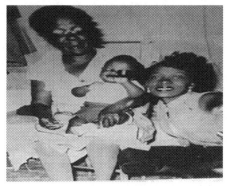

Our Family

Our family was large and full of rich history. I was always eager to learn more about my genealogy. It helped me to cope with my self-worth. Knowing your self-worth and discovering your lineage is very important to your development. My beginning started with many uncertainties, yet I understood that God had a purpose and a plan for me. I am grateful for my beginning. I learned that it doesn't determine who you really are. I can truly say I had a village that encouraged me along the way.

I learned from the good things as well as the bad. **Romans 8:28 KJV says, "And all things work together for good to them that love God, to them who are called according to his purpose."** God had a purpose at the beginning of my life; nothing catches him by surprise. He knew my beginning, middle and my ending. He is the author and finisher of my faith. I now understand the hymn, "God specializes in things that seem impossible." In my finite mind, I felt like my life was worthless. I was unworthy to be loved, because I was different. I was rejected because I didn't have light skin, a good grain of hair, and a beautiful look according to men. Only God can show you who you really are and open the eyes of your understanding and show you your worth. *1 Samuel 16:7KJV says, "For man looks on the outward appearance, but the Lord looks on the heart."*

On this journey, I have met some attractive people. Who, in their hearts were so proud and arrogant that it took away from the outward and inward beauty? I have since learned and accepted that God beautifies the meek with salvation. Whatever you do, please do not despise your beginnings. I am honored that God took me and he made something beautiful out of my life. He took a wretch like me and showed his loving concern and by his grace, he made my life a new and better one. I owe him my everything. I am thankful for the parents he chose for me. I thank him for the mountains and valley I had to experience at the beginning of my life.

I Thank him for the fire of rejection, the fire of persecution, and the fire of self-sabotage. I may have some scars, but I don't smell like what I've been through. The fire of my beginning could not burn what the Lord had destined for my life.

What is rejection? It's the act of not accepting, believing, or considering something. Rejection is a weapon the enemy uses to keep us from reaching our fullest potential. The enemy comes to steal kill and destroy us all. The fire of persecution is meant to attack our character. If we believe the lies of the adversary it will cause us to retreat. Jesus is our example he was called Beelzebub, yet he continued to be about his Father's business.

The fire of self-sabotage is when we hinder our own success. We set ourselves up for failure by believing the negative words that were spoken over our lives. We have to stop rehearsing what was said negatively about us and believe the word of God. Life and death are in the power of our tongue. We must speak a word of life over our circumstances. I had to learn how to renounce things that were spoken over me and the things people have released in the atmosphere and send it back to the lake of fire. It was his consuming fire of the word of God that transformed my life and now I am becoming the vessel that was once void and empty into the one who is now redefined and filled with his Spirit.

My beginning was necessary for my development; like Moses, my destiny was already predestined.

Food for Thought

What has your beginning been like?

Don't allow it to stop you from achieving your God-given dreams or goals.

Fiery trials are meant to make us strong. Don't allow your negative beginning to burn your desires to be all that God created you to be. Let the Lord change your story.

Press toward the mark of the prize of the high calling in Christ Jesus.

CHAPTER 2
IDENTITY CRISIS

I dentity is who you are purposed to be. An identity crisis is a period of uncertainty and confusion in which a person's sense of identity becomes uncertain. I was told Garland Walker was my father. However, the DNA was not compatible. I had no resemblance, and I knew something was missing. I had so many questions. Who was I? Was I adopted? Did I get abandoned? Why was I so dark? The list went on and on.

When a person is in an identity crisis trying to be someone or something they are not, it is devastating and challenging. That individual becomes an imposter. It's like trying to fit a circle into a square; no matter how hard you try to fit; you still end up hurting yourself and you will never fit unless you conform to what others want you to be.

The saddest part is that you devalue yourself and lose your self-worth.

Transformation is a process; it takes time to evolve into the person that God created us to be. ***Psalms 51:5KJV states, Behold, I was shapened in iniquity; and in sin did my mother conceive me.***

At the beginning of time, God knew we would need a Savior to reveal who he created us to be. I did not know who I was, so I was lost in a world of uncertainties, searching for love. During this search for love, my innocence was taken away from me and misused. This can leave someone broken and feeling empty. I was surrounded by individuals who stated that they loved and cared for me; however, their love had stipulations. When love carries stipulations it is not love it is manipulation.

The stages of the butterfly best describe this process. In my identity crisis period, I was in a cocoon. I was isolated from who God created me to be. I limited my worth based on those around me and allowed them to dictate to me my capabilities. I valued their opinions and I trusted that they had my best interest at hand, only to find out differently.

I thought I was being protected and in a safe place; however, in that place, I lost myself trying to be what everyone wanted me to be. The transformation process can either make you or break you. It almost destroyed me. The transformation process is shedding off the old self and becoming a new creature. In order to shed away the weights that easily beset us we must first acknowledge what the weights are. We must learn to listen to our innermost feelings. I often desired more out of life. I would always say, "I am going to be somebody". I had to go through some challenging obstacles to come to a place of discovery. I am grateful for the yearning inside of me that keeps me striving and thriving for something more.

There is a hero inside each one of us. We must discover the hero inside of ourselves. The greatest hero is us. When we put people on a pedestal, we can easily become prey to their demands. I lost my identity to people who said they loved me; however, they were only using me. Although, I did not know it at the time, the greater inside of me was working things out for my good. I am grateful for my transformation process. As painful as it was, I overcame it but it was a process.

The caterpillar stage is the feeding process. Depending on what we are fed determines the next stage. I can remember the words of my grandmother. She told me to finish school, don't get pregnant out of wedlock, and I would be very special. I fed off those words. Those words were my driving force. I was determined to make her proud of me. My internal struggle with the guilt of being taken advantage of left me in torment, in addition to being molested, it did not stop me. I was determined to overcome whatever obstacles I faced. I was very good at masking and performing. I did what I had to do to be accepted. I called it survival mode.

I was taught not to talk about disgraceful things like being sexually abused. When you talk about these things it brings disgrace and shame to the individual. The avoidance game has caused such trauma in the lives of so many people. Today, the victim becomes the culprit especially if you reveal it. We are taught to act as if it never happened. The offender is often justified. This method has caused a lot of individuals to lose their identity. The Identity crisis causes you to conform to a person God never intended you to be. People don't like to talk about why females and males get involved in alternate lifestyles. This is an identity crisis. The reason it occurs is because of the violation that has taken place in their lives, and they never have the opportunity to heal from the trauma.

The Pupa Transition stage is where I had to grow up and accept that I had issues. It was a painful process. I had to admit to the mental and physical abuse that left me with an identity crisis. When a person is abused to this magnitude, it causes them to internalize things. I developed self-esteem issues, inferiority complexes and I developed fabrication issues. The fabrication became a big issue. I wanted so badly to be accepted that I would make up stories to make my life appear better than it was. This caused me some significant relationships.

The final stage is the adult stage, where maturity, formality, and acceptance occur. The song, "The greatest love of all", says it all. I had to learn to love myself and I had to accept the things I couldn't change and change the things I could. I had to forgive myself and accept that people could not give me what they did not have. The statement, Hurt people hurt people," is so true. I couldn't make people accept me. I had to learn to love myself first before I could truly love anyone else. The greatest love is learning to love yourself. As a child, I wanted the light skin, the curly hair, the small lips. In other words, I want to be a barbie doll.

I tried to change who God created me to be by hanging with the in-crowd. It resulted in me lowering my standards to be accepted and allowing individuals to take advantage of me mentally and physically. Being different has its pros and cons. It really depends on the individuals and their surroundings. A lot of the stereotyping caused me a lot of heartaches and mental anguish, resulting in an identity crisis. I was often picked on and called names because of my hair, skin color and looks. When one has an identity crisis, they have the tendency to do things to be accepted. The bible says, "Death and life are in the power of the tongue and those who love it will eat the fruit." (Proverbs 18:21)

Many negative words were spoken over me, such as. "You are too black, you are ugly, you are a bald-headed black snake and many other degrading names; however, the fire of those negative words could not burn the dignity inside me. Once I learned to love myself and who God created me to be, I was transformed. I learned how to do my hair, makeup and my dress apparel was enhanced. I was placed in the path of friends who encouraged me and helped me build my self-esteem outwardly. However, I still dealt with my internal struggle of not really knowing my self-worth. The internal struggle can be daunting; it can make you feel unlovable, unworthy, and confused. This led me down a path of performance uncertainties, and false hopes. Although people told me how beautiful I was, it was hard to believe it. My outward appearance changed, yet, inwardly I felt condemnation and clueless about who I was and what I was capable of being.

It is not until we allow the Holy Spirit to take full reign over our lives that growth and development will take place. I often hear people say things like I am going to change my life. The problem is when we change our lives the fix is only temporal. However, when Christ changes our lives, it is eternal. The moral of the story is that you can fix your outward appearance, but, until you believe in yourself, you will continue lacking self-esteem.

Although I struggled with who I was the fire of an identity crisis could not burn my self-worth. I am so grateful that my identity was not in my lack of confidence; that would have been devastating.

The New Living Translations of Psalms 139:14 says it best - Thank you for making me so wonderfully complex! Your workmanship is marvelous- how well I know it. God created me to be more than a conqueror.

What Identity Crisis are you struggling with?

Christ made us overcomers through his word.

If I can do it, so can you.

Use your God-given courage to surmount and soar like an eagle.

CHAPTER 3
BOY MEETS GIRL

Me and My Dad

At the age of 7yrs old, I found out who my biological father was. My life forever changed. I finally discovered who this big black Santa Claus was. I truly believe that my grandmother was trying to make up for the mistakes she made with my mother. I would occasionally hear my grandmother and mother disagreeing. My grandmother would tell Addie she needed to know who her father was. My father was always around; I wasn't aware he was my father. I thought he was my uncle for a long time. He would always appear when I was in dire need of clothing, new shoes, or he would randomly come by to see my grandmother. He was called boy Bryant. His real name was Avery Bryant. My grandmother Mamie said his nickname was because he stayed in a lot of trouble because of his outspokenness. She would get mad and say boy sit down or boy do this or that. My grandmother Hattie finally convinced my mother to let me spend time with him over the summer months. The agreement was I was not supposed to know he was my father. My father was staying with his first cousin Sadie.

I can remember that day so vividly. He taught me table manners and how to say my grace before eating during breakfast. I asked him Uncle Boy, please pass me the butter and Sadie looked at me and said, "Uncle Boy," girl! He's is not your uncle; that's your father." My eyes got big, like a fifty-cent coin and it was complete silence at the table. She proceeded to tell me can't you see, you look just like him, my father got angry with her and said Sadie, Addie is going to be mad. Her response was I don't care. This baby needs to know the truth.

At that very moment, my whole world changed. My identity was revealed and a void in my life was filled. I then understood why I looked different from my other siblings, and I was happy to know that I belonged. I will never forget my father's response when I said, Daddy, please pass the butter," he began to cry.

When I returned home, I was excited to let everyone know that Uncle Boy was my father, I was in for a rude awakening. My mother was not very pleased, and she scolded me for calling him, daddy. Although my emotions were one of excitement. I had many questions like why did my mother hide this from me? How much better my life could have been if I had known my biological father from the beginning?

Why did she hate me so much? I had a flood of emotions. This hurt me deeply. I felt like I was being punished by her.

My early years were robbed of having a father figure in my life because my mother had some unresolved issues with him. I was told he denied me at birth and her expectations was for me to deny him, how could I? The missing piece to the puzzle in my life had come together. I didn't care what he'd done. All that mattered to me is I had a father. I was just so excited about discovering him. My identity was revealed. In my mind, I felt like the prodigal son. I was lost and now I was found. I was finally receiving the love I longed for. The more time I spent with my father, the more I learned about my family genealogy. I understood why my great aunts showed me so much love and favoritism. My father was very well known, and he was highly respected. My father's uncle John was Aunt Earline's husband and Sadie was their daughter. This made me double kin on both sides of the family through marriage; Uncle John was her father, making my dad her first cousin.

I loved spending the summer with Cousin Sadie and her family. Her daughter Chiquita would do my hair and her sons were like big brothers to me. My father spent a lot of time over at my Aunt Pudding's house, and he would share his heart with her and of course, she would tell my grandmother.

My grandmother always used stories to encourage me. One of my favorite fairy tales was the Ugly Duckling. She used the illustration of how the ugly duckling was different from the others because he was special, just like me. She told me I would grow up and be a beautiful swan. My father was eager for me to meet his side of the family in South Carolina.

My experience was like a dream come true. When I saw my first cousins and the strong resemblance we had, it was like I was looking in a mirror. We had so many attributes alike. I felt a sense of belonging. I am ever grateful for the role my father played in my life. I am a firm believer every child needs that father figure in their life. My father made up for lost time. He made sure I received all the love and nurturing I needed. I have so many fond memories. I remember when he took me out on a lunch date. He would explain to me how a young man should treat a beautiful young lady like myself. He would open my car door, pull my chair out and push it in once I was seated. He always made sure he helped me with my coat. My father always told me how beautiful and special I was to him and God. He made sure I attended church every Sunday.

My father was on the usher's board at the church. He was one of the sharpest ushers I have ever seen. He did not play when it came to talking in church or chewing gum in the sanctuary. It was if he had a radar, and he would catch me every time I was chewing gum with my friends. His goal was to train me in the admonition of the Lord. Although there were areas in his life that he struggled with, I can truly say I saw the transformation in his life. He taught me how to pray and he taught me how to love. He made me feel very special. I was his beautiful daughter. My parents had similar situations in their life in reference to their childhood. My dad was not educated. He was a hard worker. He achieved many things and he let nothing stop him. He taught himself how to read and drive tractors, eighteen-wheelers and heavy constructions equipment. I loved our road trips. He would use those trips to teach me the ins and outs of driving and expose me to traveling the world. He was raised in the south and he told me once the boys reached a certain age, they were not allowed to finish school. They were given to a slave master to harvest the fields. He was big on getting your education. My father was a very outspoken person. He was a very fast learner and very proud. It was years before I knew he couldn't read or write well. He was the backbone of his family. Everyone looked up to him. He was very strict and had very high expectations for many of us. He taught me how to drive and he made sure I got my driver's education completed to get my learner's permit. He gave me my very first car. Our family was his world. He made sure I learned about my family on both sides. We had a routine when I would visit him for the summer. He would teach me how to cook his favorite meals. He helped me develop my gift of praying because we prayed when we got up, when we traveled, and before bed. I guess that's why I love to pray.

My father played a very instrumental role in my spiritual upbringing. I had to be in church every Sunday, starting with Sunday school. I loved our family church, Galilee Baptist Church. It was there I discovered my gift to sing. We had a very strong youth department. The highlight of going to church with him was spending time with my Uncle Clarence and Aunt Missy after church services. Our church was very active; we would have two to three services every Sunday. I loved the choirs; all of them could sing, from the youth choir, young adult choir, and senior choir. Our family church was a very charismatic.

My father loved to dress, and he made sure I was dressed nicely as well. He always wanted a son; however, God saw fit to give him all daughters. He would get advice from Aunt

Pudding, Sadie, and Minnie Lee on how to dress me. My favorite fashion designer was Minnie. I loved when she came to visit her mother, Aunt Pudding. She was a very flamboyant dresser. I loved how she dressed. My father would have Minnie go with him to the store called Morton's in DC to get my Sunday clothing. Minnie would pick the most colorful dresses, but she would have me looking nice. My father couldn't do my hair, so he would get family members like Chiquita to braid my hair. He really made sure I looked my best. One thing about my father I admired was how he never gave me anything without making sure my siblings had things as well. At times I didn't like that because I really did not want to share him.

There was nothing I couldn't ask my father for. He wanted me to know that he was available and did not have to fear talking to him about anything. I'm so grateful for a God-fearing father his words of wisdom showed me the way and path I should take. I witnessed him maturing in the things of God. He became a living example for all of us.

My father was a generational curse breaker, and he passed the mantle on to me. He left a legacy that money could not buy, knowing Christ and having a personal relationship with him. The validation of a father in a child's life is very important. The daughter's sense of self is closely tied to her relationship with her father. He affirms her by encouraging, nurturing and being a strong male role model in her life. His role is to demonstrate love, compassion, and comfort. He is her provider, protector, and confidant. This is a type and shadow of Christ. The earthly father plays a major role in the lives of his children. He is the determining factor in their lives.

However, if the earthly father is absent, then our Heavenly Father is there to fill in the missing pieces because he loves us. He is our protector, provider, and confidant. He came to seek and save the lost. His desire is to validate us. He is known as the comforter. When one meets Christ, their life is changed. Their identity is revealed, and generational curses are broken. It's then, the fire of not knowing who your biological parents are isn't any longer an issue; however, it is a steppingstone to your healing and development.

Although my earthly father came into my life, there were still areas in my life that he could not fill. It was the introduction of my Heavenly Father that brought total restoration. The scars of the years of not knowing my real father impacted my life. They resulted in me not having healthy relationships with men. In addition, I had to release the unforgiveness I had towards my mother. The devil wanted me to hold on to the hurt and unforgiveness. I am grateful that the Lord's convictions from his word freed me. ***Matthew 6: 14KJV states, for if ye forgive men their trespasses, your heavenly Father will also forgive you.***

Once I forgave both my parents my life changed. The residue of the abandonment was removed and by the grace of God. The fire of my father being absent at the beginning of my life could not burn my desire to have a relationship with my biological father. He came at a time when I needed him most. He was the one that introduced me to my Heavenly Father.

Proverbs 22:6 KJV says, "Train up a child in the way he should go: and when he is old, he will not depart from it."

You may not now your earthly father and this has left you feeling empty.

However, the heavenly Father wants to feel that void.

On June 23,2018 the title of my first book was given by the Holy Spirit.

The Fire couldn't burn me.

There are two types of fires I would like to talk about. The first fire that is meant to destroy and God's consuming Fire. The consuming fire burns up the limitations we have in God.

Fire- combustion or burning, in which substance combine chemically with oxygen from the air and typically give out bright light, heat and smoke. Fire in its most common form can result in configuration which has the potential to cause physical damage

Consuming fire utterly consumes or destroys anything unholy. This fire refines and purifies. It removes limitations

(F-Formula) (I-Ignited) (R- relinquish) (E- Excuses)

The second fire equals trials, tribulations or temptations that we deal with on a regular basis. The consuming fire is what Moses experienced with the burning bush. God's fire removed the limitations Moses had and gave him the unlimited power of God to execute the Will of God for his life.

At the beginning of my life, I faced many obstacles. I was raised by a single mother until I reached the age of seven. I had a complex about my skin color and my natural features. I was made fun of because I was different, and it caused me to have self-esteem issues.

Fire can destroy if not extinguished in time. However, God is a consuming fire, and His word will accomplish that which He sent it out to do.

CHAPTER 4
THE CONSUMING FIRE

T he enemy uses fires to destroy the lives of many people. The tongue also is a fire, a world of evil among the parts of the body. It corrupts the whole person, sets the whole course on a deadly fire. The fire of negative words, the fire of deception, the fire of loneliness, the fire of jealousy and the list can go on and on. However, God desires to consume those fires in our lives. These can be the chaffs in our lives, but God said, **"Blessed is the man that walketh not in the counsel of the ungodly nor standeth in the way of sinners, nor sitteth in the seat of the scornful, but his delight is in the law of the Lord, and in his law doth he meditate day and night, and he shall be like a tree that is planted by the rivers of water that bringeth forth his fruit in his season in his leaf also shall not wither, and whatsoever he doeth shall prosper" (Psalms 1:1-3)KJV** So, we all know that a fire has the potential of destroying the leaves, whether they are green or dry. However, when God is in the fire, it will not be able to destroy us. God desires to give us beauty for ashes. He even told us in his word that the fire shall not Kindle upon us, nor will the waters overtake us.

We must trust the promises of God. The Lord desires to write a new chapter in our lives. It's not over until God says that it is over. In life, many fiery trials came to consume me. The trial of life makes us doubt if there is a God. Some people are still living in the past because the fires of the negative words that were spoken over them as a child still consumes them.. This has resulted in them not being able to thrive. I was inspired by the Holy Spirit to write this book to encourage you that life goes on and with Christ as the head, You, in all things, are more than conquerors and we shall surmount. What the enemy meant to destroy you with, God is using it as a platform to encourage others. It's not how you start but it's how you finish.

God allows fire in our lives to burn up our limitations. The fire is to make us shine so that others may see our heavenly Father's good works and glorify him. From the beginning, Satan said, "I would never amount to anything. However, the author and the finisher of my faith said otherwise. Years later, I am walking out my destiny, sharing my story of how God took a little girl born in Washington DC. He made something beautiful out of her life. He turned my ashes into beauty. That's why the fire of rejection, the fire of misuse, the fire of divorce, the fire of betrayal, the fire of persecution did not burn me; it only made me stronger, and I give him praise.

There is absolutely nothing too hard for God. Jehovah Rapha is the God that heals; he can take the scars from a fire and engraft new life. ***If any man be in Christ, he is new creature old things are passed away and behold he makes all things new (2 Cor. 5:17.)KJV*** Now I walk with the King, I pray to the King, and see results because I am a child of the King.

I am so glad Christ left such a great cloud of witnesses to be my example. The master-builder can make you over and let you start with a new beginning. The Hebrew boys came out of the flame, not smelling like smoke. If the Lord, did it for the Hebrew boys and me, he could do it for you! Take the limits off.

CHAPTER 5
GENERATIONAL CURSE

A generational curse is believed to be passed down from one generation to another due to rebellion against God. The family lineage is marked by divorce, incest, poverty, anger, alcoholism, or other ungodly patterns, this is most likely generational curses.

The Bible says that these curses are tied to choices.

***Deuteronomy 30:19*NIV says, "We can either choose life and blessing or death and cursing.**

We inherit many traits and preferences from our parents that aren't always a positive influence on ourselves or others. Our sinful habits or beliefs can negatively affect our lives and those around us. It is very important to know your family genealogy. Generational curses are real and can be passed down to the next generation if not dealt with. We all carry our parental genetics. There are certain characteristics about both my parents that I loved and certain characteristics that I hated. My mother was a single parent raising 5 children. I was the youngest of the five.

My mother was a hard worker; she had a lot of tenacity. She never gave up without a fight. She was a strong-willed individual. She did not allow any obstacles to define her or limit her from accomplishing her dreams. She kept trying until she reached her goals no matter what. I observed her going to work, never missing a day, rain, shine, sleet or hail, unless she was extremely ill. When it snowed, she would walk miles to work to provide for us. She made many sacrifices for her family, some good and some not so good. I watched her deal with a lot of regrets. My mom desired the genuine love that she often gave to others, but it was not reciprocated at times.

I remember a conversation she and I had after the death of her brother and her mother. She told me how at an early age, she was given in marriage because she became pregnant as a teenager. She said her mother never educated her about how children were conceived. My grandmother told her babies came from the cabbage patch. She learned the hard way that is not how it happens. So, at an early age, her life was changed drastically. It was a shame to have children out of wedlock in those days. She had to marry and because marriages then were sacred, you had to get married in a different color dress if you were not a virgin. She said she was made to wear a light blue dress, so everyone knew she was with child. I later learned my grandmother had a child out of wedlock as well. The only difference is her baby's father died before she could marry him. Generational curses will be passed down unless someone desires to make a difference. My grandmother would often share with me her mistakes, but I believe it was pride that would not allow her to apologize to my mom. I believe it would have made a great difference in my mother's life.

My mother shared with me that she was treated differently from her other sisters. She dealt with the same stereotyping and rejection I dealt with. She was rejected and ridiculed because she was different. The curse of pregnancy out of wedlock was passed down from one generation to another. The curse of alcoholism was passed down from generation to generation. My grandmother got pregnant out of wedlock, then my mother, my sisters and I got pregnant out of wedlock. I witnessed members of my family that died from sclerosis of the liver. It was the by the grace of God that my life addiction with drugs and alcohol did not destroy me. When I look back over my life, I know it was the hand of God on my life. I was considered a functioning alcoholic. I masked it well. I was fortunate to recognize I needed help. My grandmother did the best she could with the knowledge that was given her, and my mother did the best she could as well. I am forever grateful that they kept striving even during their mistakes and struggles. I often thought about how my mother could have aborted me but she didn't. She had dignity and she kept her family together to the best of her ability. I was glad I was able to apologize to her and make things right before she left this earth. I see so much of her in myself now that I am older.

My desire was not to become the by-product of my environment. However, that which I tried so hard to avoid, which was our generational curse, I found myself headed in that same direction. I realized my grandmother did to my mother the same thing that was done to me. The verbal, physical, and mental abuse caused me so much anguish. I held resentment in my heart for a long time because I felt that my mother didn't love me. I witnessed my mother hiding her pain in the alcohol bottle and relationships that left her unsatisfied. Drinking was a generational curse in our family. It was a form of escape for many. I also followed the pattern of hiding my problems behind the bottle and drugs. However, In the midst of my mother's challenges she pursued her dreams.

She always wanted to be a nurse; however, being a young mother with five children, it was hard to attend college and fulfill her heart's desires. We learned from her genuine work ethic. My mother was a go-getter. She never gave up. She finally went to school after we were grown and on our own to achieve her nursing degree. Despite how many times she failed the test, she did not stop until she received her LPN. I have that same ambition as her to work in the medical field. I am now 25 years in the field of dialysis. I am honored to have inherited this positive generational trait from my mother. I am determining to be the agent of change in my family legacy. I am that curse breaker. I found out people are afraid to expose the curses in their family for the fear of rejections. I am grateful that the Lord has set me free from the opinions of men. There is a song that states, If you wanna be somebody, if you wanna go somewhere, you better wake up and pay attention.

We teach our children what we have been taught unless we take it upon ourselves to do better. I remember when I became sexually active, I was so afraid to share with my mother for fear of her response. My grandmother signed my consent form to get birth control pills. I tried to hide my pills and my mother went on one of her cleaning raids and found them. Just what I feared came to pass. I was scolded and made to feel ashamed because I was sexually active. I thought she would have been proud that I was being responsible and being proactive. The scenario was different, but the outcome was the same. She did not educate me about sex and its pros and cons. I learned from friends, and I remember reading a book called Dear God it's me Margaret by Judy Blume. The avoidance technique was very strong. The scripture is so true, **"My people perish because of lack of knowledge." (Hosea 4:6)** KJV I received Christ; the Holy Spirit revealed to me that my mother couldn't give me what she never received. I vowed that my children would not experience the things that I experienced as a child. I vowed that they would have the same parents so that they would not be treated differently, and God granted me my desire. I prayed that my daughter would know what real love is. *(1John 4:7-21KJV) says, "God is love."* I can say she has a personal relationship with Christ. I prayed that my son would break the generational curse and the stigma that comes with single parents raising young men and that has come to pass. I found myself following in the same footsteps of my parents. I had sex outside of marriage. I got pregnant without being married. However, my firstborn did not survive. My father tried to instill the principle of waiting until marriage. Yet, it was hard for me to adhere when he was involved in relationships without being married. I know generational curses are meant to be broken. The Lord is looking for willing vessels to say yes and trust his process. I am determined to be the agent of change in my family's legacy. I am that curse breaker. I found out people are afraid to expose the curses in their family for the fear of rejections. I am grateful that the Lord has set me free from the opinion of men. The change in our lives cannot happen unless we first acknowledge the issues that are hindering our deliverance.

Our lifestyles are a choice. As I learned about my family's history on both sides, there were characteristics I desired and characteristics I denounced, and I am still denouncing. My father was not able to obtain an education. His desire was for my siblings, me, and his grandchildren to obtain greater knowledge. I am on that path to do greater works than my ancestors. The bible tells us greater works shall they do. I can see the fruit of his prayers working even in my old age. I am pursuing an education. The fire of limitation is not burning my will to do greater works than my forefathers. The fire of generational curses could not burn me.

Are you duplicating your family's generational curses?

Who haven't you forgiven?

You are a Change Agent?

Your destiny lies within you.

(1 John 4:4NIV) "Ye are of God, little children, and have overcome them: because greater is he that is in you, than he that is in the world."

CHAPTER 6
SEARCHING FOR LOVE

I n my senior year, I was in the class of 1983. I graduated with honors. I took the postal exam passed it with a high score. However, I wanted to get away from the dysfunction I saw in my everyday life. I was engaged but unsure if I was ready to marry right out of high school. I went to South Carolina to meet my father's side of the family. The words that I spoke in chapter one became a reality. I met several individuals interested in a long-term relationship with me. However, I was not ready. After two unsuccessful engagements, I finally met the one I thought was the man I would spend the rest of my life with. He had all the qualities of my earthly father. He was a provider, he was family-oriented, yet one quality was missing he did not know how to express love and affection. The first several years were blissful. He introduces me to a better way of living. I didn't want for anything except genuine love. I called it the honeymoon stage. I thought I had found my soulmate. I got pregnant with our first son out of wedlock. That was something I vowed never to do. My father was very disappointed in me. In my fifth month, I had a miscarriage. I can identify with any woman who carries a child and then lose it. It is a very heartbreaking situation. This caused me to go into a deep depression. Later that year, we got married.

The first word I spoke in chapter one became a reality. I was now Mrs. Jones. Then came our second-born Jarod Avery, named after my father and then our daughter Phaedra Monique. My second spoken word became a reality. I said I was going to have two children and I did. Now I can see the handwriting on the wall. It was a gift given to me that I had not discovered yet. We had the materialistic things, and he was an amazing father to them but faithfulness to me was an issue. Our lives together were one thing in the public eye but privately, it lacked so much. We both were very immature, and we had no clue what it took to make a marriage work.

The partying, the drinking and drugs did not help matters. My search for love caused me to stay longer than I should of and accept things that I was unacceptable; mental abuse, verbal abuse and physical abuse became my new norm.

One thing about love is that it does leave bruises. Bruises are not just physical, but they can be mental. I suffered more mental abuse than anything. I stayed as long as I did because I did not want to hear my father say I told you not to marry. The second reason was I wanted it to work because my whole life, I saw nothing but marriages fail in my family. Third, I wanted my children to have a real family. I was determined to prove a point that I made the right decision. I wanted my children to have that functional family with a mother and father under the same. I did not want them to deal with the things I dealt with as a child having a different father. In this search for love, I put myself and my children in some compromising situations. I ignored the red flags hoping for the best.

When our finances became depleted due to misuse, it was then I experienced the most painful rejection. Mental abuse was the tool used to keep me in bondage. In the beginning, he was ok with taking care of everything. Of course, I felt like this is what real love is; the man is the provider. He had a good job; however, when the gambling addiction took place, the ball game changed. The love that I thought I had come to a painful end. I endured betrayal, lies and abandonment. My earthly father saw these things coming but I tried to cover them up from him. The saying that your parents know when their children are going through is so true.

My father knew the pain and suffering I was enduring. I remember him saying he felt his son-in-law was living a double life. Of course, I denied it because my pride did not want to hear the words, I told you so. I tried to cover up our financial problems however our debts continued to spiral downward we was facing bankruptcy. I always had a backup plan which was my father. If we got into a financial bind, I could rely on him. I finally had to grow up and learn how to figure things out on my own. I stopped leaning so much on my father's love for my children and me and dealt with doing without. I had to discover what real love was and what it wasn't. I recognized that my father was going through financially and getting older. His health was failing, so I decided not to be a burden on him anymore. When things got unbearable, I found myself hiding behind drugs, alcohol and unhealthy relationships resulting in my self-esteem being damaged. I wanted this love so bad that I put all my hopes and dreams on the back burner to try and keep up an image that was a lie. In the process of this, I lost myself. My dreams were to attend school and become a nurse. However, I had to forfeit that dream because I became a wife and mother at an early age.

CHAPTER 7
THE FIRE OF REJECTION

I n the south, working at certain jobs gave you prestige and power. The love of money, power and prestige determined your worth. The money-making plants were Savannah River Plant, Kimberly Clark and Salem Carpet. He worked at Savannah River Plant, and I was often called names because I would not apply for a job there. When I spoke of my dreams to go back to school for nursing, it was frowned upon. I worked for Salem Carpet, yet that was considered a low-class job. When the love from a mortal man failed me, I wanted to end my own life. I had friends, but I soon realized their purpose was only friends with benefits and I was always paying the ultimate price. I would always go the extra mile hoping that in return, I would receive that same love, not so. I had to finally realize people cannot give you want they don't have. The more I drank, the more depressed

I became; nothing could numb the pain of the rejection I was feeling. When I was young, my dad kept me in the church, so godly values and principles were instilled in me. I just ignored them because I thought I knew a better way. *Train up a child in the way they should go when they grow old, they will not depart. (Proverbs 22:6).* KJV I found out the hard way. *Proverbs 13.15NIV Good understanding giveth favor: but the way of the transgressor is hard.* I realized the search for love stemmed from my rejection when I was a child. I always wanted to be accepted. At times I felt I never measured up. I watched family members stay in abusive situations that later resulted in painful outcomes. I realized that if the foundation of love is not properly laid, your life will result in a faulty foundation.

I ran away from what I thought was dysfunctional, only to end up in a more devastating situation. I learned as a little girl what love was not. I have seen so much unfaithfulness, abuse, and neglect. The world says love is people, places and things. However, the greatest love is Jesus Christ. I was so caught up in the tradition of religion and church that my ears were dull to the word that could have liberated me. I connected with people who were just like me; it was a mirage, and I based the love that I was searching for on what I had. One thing I learned is that hurting people hurt people. I had the house, cars, financial stability but I did not have the love. I had what society said love was. There were times I went to friends for advice, and it appeared that their home was functional and filled with love. I found that to be a lie. My surroundings were filled with people who ran rail for rail. The words of wisdom given to me were not what I needed to hear. I was told it was ok to find love in others when you weren't receiving it at home. However, I knew in my heart that was not right. The four-letter word love is so powerful. However, love without substance or meaning is just mere words.

I loved love songs, especially from Luther Vandross. He was one of my favorite R&B artists. "A house is not a home" was my theme song. I would get drunk and listen to that song and just cry. I had two children and I was clueless about how to raise them. I purposely poured my love into them. They became my reason to keep going. Most of the time, it was them and me. We had to always compete with the liquor house or the fellows or the gambling house. The only time we looked like a lovely family was during the holidays. We dressed the part; we looked the part, but we were so far apart. I tried so desperately to keep up with this image. The more I tried, the worst it became.

CHAPTER 8
THE DAY OF DELIVERANCE

One day I came to a crossroads in my life. I will always be grateful to Minnie Lee Smith. I found myself drinking in the morning, noonday, and night to escape my pain. I would go by her house every day after work. It was my place of refuge. My cousin could make you laugh. She always made sure dinner was cooked and we would sit down and eat and talk. I never knew she paid close attention to my behavior. On this day, I stopped by the store to get my usual drink. I normally would drink it before I got to her house but I had a double and brought it into her house. She looked at me and these were her words, "What are you doing?" Are you going to be an alcoholic like the rest of the family? Those words pierced my heart like a knife. I never heard her scold me before. She never said anything out of the way to me. She then began to encourage me. She said you are a beautiful young lady; don't you allow anyone to cause you to destroy yourself because they don't know what they have. She told me I reminded her of herself when she was younger with young children. She let me know that she was there for the children and me and that I was going to be alright. Then she cracked a joke and asked if I needed to go to rehab and I told her no, I was going to be alright.

Those words she spoke provoked me to cry out to God for deliverance. I did not want to be a repeat offender of our generation. I wanted to be different. The love I was searching for was not in the bottle, the drugs or the relationships; however, it was in Christ. I can identify with the song, "I searched all over, I looked high and low, couldn't find nobody greater." I needed to be healed from my beginning. The spirit of rejection caused me to accept whatever came my way to fill the void that was only meant to be filled by the Lord. He allowed me to come to a low place, this place caused me to cry out to him. It is nothing worse than searching for something of value and not being able to find it. The fire of drugs, alcohol, broken relationships could not burn my search for genuine love.

What are you searching for?

The search is over.

Look to the Author and Finisher of your Faith

Hebrew 12:2 KJV Looking unto Jesus the Author and finisher of our faith,

CHAPTER 9
THE ENCOUNTER-MY SALVATION

September 22,1989 is the year hurricane Hugo hit Charleston SC. It was also the year I gave my heart to the Christ. My life was in turmoil so I could relate to this storm. Things were so chaotic. I didn't know if I was coming or going. My marriage was in turmoil, I was hiding behind alcohol and drugs to numb the pain of rejection from my husband. I found out he was having an extra marital affair so I figured I would get even so I went outside of my marriage for fulfillment. I found out God always has a Nathan to let you know that your sins will surely find you out. Sin can lead you down the wrong path if left undealt with. I realized how much God loved me. He sent his handmaiden to witness to me and let me know what I was doing would not solve anything. The answer to my situation was not what I wanted to hear at that time. The answer was Jesus. I had the form of Godliness, but I denied his delivering power. I made a bunch of excuses I felt I was justified. He was hurting me, so I had the right to retaliate. I thought because I went to church every second and fourth Sunday I was saved, and God understood me, and he forgave me. I was a tithe payer and I sung on the mass choir. However, I lived a double life like so many people. I was singing myself to the lake of fire, drinking myself to the lake of fire and committing adultery going straight to the lake of fire in my Jesus Name. I had some friends who were my enablers. *1 Corinthians 15:33NIV Do not be misled "Bad company corrupts good character".* The English Standard Version say it best, *"Do not be deceived "Bad company ruins good morals."*

I knew better, yet listening to the wrong advice stirred me down the road of destruction. I thought if I repented and ask forgiveness everything would be alright. The thing I didn't understand was each time I willfully sinned I picked up seven demons worst then the ones I already had. I couldn't understand each time I felt worse and worse. How many times I would ask for forgiveness and then become a repeat offender. I never forget how God's grace drew me. I was going to see some male strippers with my girlfriends, we had snorted cocaine and was drinking the more I indulge the less effective the narcotics and alcohol became. When we got to the club I started dancing and it felt like I had two left feet. I knew something wasn't right because I was an excellent dancer. I thought I got ahold of some bad stuff. I sat at the bar, and I heard this voice say what are you doing here? I looked around and it was only me sitting there. I thought I was hallucinating. I had plans to meet my male friend that night as well and when we met up, I couldn't go through with it. I told him I can't do this anymore. When God's hand is on your life you can run but you can't hide. It was Gods' love drawing me out of the web of sin.

The bible says, ***"Love covers all sins," Proverbs 10:12.*** God's love was covering me even in my mess. The straw that broke the caramel back was when I was driving home that night and the power in the car went out and car cut off in the middle of the road. It was a dark road I couldn't see I was so scared. I went into religious prayer mode. It's that prayer that we do when we know we are in error, so we pray to ask the Lord to deliver us or help us and we flat out lie that if he does, we won't do it again. This time around the Lord made sure I keep my vow to him. I remember getting home safely because a nice man stopped to help me. When I got in the house, I just wanted to end it all. I was completely miserable. I sat on the sofa I had some cocaine, and some prescription pain pills. I decided to kill myself it would be the best way out of my misery. I remember saying this words Lord if you are real, please save me. He answered my prayer, and he had an angel by the name of Alfreda Bush assigned to make sure I gave my life over to him. I must have passed out I heard this loud knock at my door, and it was Minister Bush. I am forever grateful for her obedience to the Lord. She said she was on her way to Walmart and the Lord told her to come see me. She shared the gospel with me, and I accepted Christ and my life has not been the same since. I cried for hours. I remember calling my dad and saying daddy, I am saved. He said he knew because he had been fasting and praying, asking the Lord to save his daughters.

The more I cried, the lighter I felt. I experience the power of God in a supernatural way. I felt this warm heat go all over my body and his presence overshadowed me. I now know it was a cleansing and purification taking place. On this day, I became a new creature in Christ and old things were passed away. I finally realized I needed a savior to rescue me from myself. I often said I could stop if I wanted to but that was the lie, I told myself.

I opened so many portals and didn't know how to close them. The Lord grants each of us a self-will. He is a gentleman; he will not force himself on anyone. However, he will always allow us to become sick and tired of the mental and physical anguish. I was tired and exhausted from living a lie. Once I accepted him, he took the yoke of bondage from me and taught me how to learn his way and my life has been transformed.

Food for thought?

Are you tired of living a lie?

Jesus is waiting with his arms stretch open wide.

If you are not saved, let this day be your day.

Roman 10:9 KJV "That if thou shalt confess with thy mouth the Lord Jesus, and shalt believe in thine heart that God hath raised him from the dead, thou shalt be saved."

YOU ARE SAVED!! Hallelujah!!!! I am rejoicing with you and so are the angels in heaven.

Welcome home.

CHAPTER 10
CONSUMING FIRE-TRIALS THAT BURNED AWAY MY LIMITATIONS

T he fire of trials burned away the limitations. Once I received Christ in my journey, I began to discover who I was as well as who he was in my life. The scripture that became a reality to me was **1 Peter 4:12KJV "Beloved, think it not strange concerning the fiery trial, which is to try you, as though some strange thing happened unto you."** My first trial had to deal with believing that God was a healer. My daughter had a high fever, and I took her to the doctor and the medication was not working; the Lord told me to lay hands on her and she recovered. The Father always gives you the answer to the test before it begins. During this process, I learned to hear the voice of God. I would read the bible for hours and ask the Lord to speak to me. My spiritual dynamic changed drastically. I went from attending the Baptist church to attending the Pentecostal church. It was totally out of my comfort zone. My family did not understand what I was doing. However, I was led by the Holy Spirit. It was through this process I was transformed from the limitations of religion to understanding what a real relationship with Christ consisted of. The word became rhema for me. I remember the very first time I heard that tiny, small voice.

I was going into my pantry, and I heard the scripture, **"*Matthew 24:44 KJV Therefore, you also must be ready, for in an hour when you least expect, the Son of Man is coming.* Are you ready?"** It startled me and I asked Lord, ready for what? Then in my journey of discovery, I began to see who he created me to be. He allowed trials and tribulations to shape me. I was called many names, the devil, root worker and the list go on and on. I had to suffer this type of persecution to be able to be delivered from the opinions of men. I was living the word. Jesus was my example, and he was teaching me how to walk in my authority and not be moved by what people would say or think about me.

I remember asking the Lord to let me be addicted to him like I was to drugs, alcohol, and illicit sex. I had to walk it out. My trials and tribulations were challenging at that time, and I often wondered why I had to be treated like an outcast after I accepted him. I found my Christian journey to be one of many obstacles. The scripture a prophet is not honored in his own country became my reality. I was mishandled because I was female minister. Many times, leaders prostituted my gifts for their own personal gain. I was lied on by people in the household of faith. I was cast out of churches because I challenged their doctrines. I finally realized that I was fellowshipping with the suffering that Jesus Christ endured. He was calling me into a higher calling. I had to denounced religion and develop a relationship with Christ. I had to endure hardship as a good soldier. I was placed in dungeons because I would have to tell people especially authority in high places thus saith the Lord and often times it was not what they wanted to hear. The rejections of man thrust me into totally reliance on Christ. At times it was a lonely road to travel. I can identify with David I had to confronted my Goliath, I had to kill the lions and the bears. I had to denounce the mantles that man wanted to place on life and allow the potter to make me over again and again. Many times, he had to reshape me and model me over.

Once I learned who I belonged to and that nothing could separate me from the love of God not even my failures even as a believer. I began to soar like that eagle. My gift always made room for me in many arenas. I recognize the Jeremiah anointing on my life. He was known as the weeping prophet. I have cried many tears because of the things I've seen and had to endure. I suffered persecution for telling the truth. *Jeremiah 1:10 NIV "See, I have this day set thee over the nations and over the kingdoms to uproot and tear down, to destroy and overthrow, to build and plant."* In order to help someone, you must first be a partaker of their suffering. I had to uproot my own issues and then allow the word of God to rebuild me in his image.

These trials and tribulations thrust me to depend on God even when I could not see him or feel him. The situation caused me to cry out to the Lord for deliverance. I was left in a foreclosed home with two children and a job making six dollars and twenty-three cents an hour. When the sheriff showed up at my home to evict my children and me, I was so afraid; however, the favor of God touched his heart and he told me I could live there until I was able to find residency elsewhere. I was accused of having sin in my life because my car was stolen, my husband left me, and the church rejected me because divorce was frowned upon.

The story of Hagar gave me the courage to persevere. I felt like her. What was I going to do? I felt like I had lost it all. I remember crying out to the Lord, telling him I wanted to die, and he used my daughter Phaedra to bring me back to reality. I asked the question, Lord, why this must happen to me? I questioned how a God could allow such pain and still love me. The pain was like one that was giving birth without an epidural. All I wanted was to be delivered. I wanted my marriage to be restored; however, the Lord had other plans. I remember him telling me that he would comfort me. Kirk Franklin's song was, "it's a blessing in the storm" was constantly ringing in my spirit. I could not see it at the time because I allowed the pain to control my emotions. I thank God for the Holy Spirit. The bible says he will lead and guide you into all truth. The truth I found was in the word of God. I have experienced some hard trials; however, the Lord showed himself mightily. Once he delivered me from them all, the fire of those trials burned away my small mind and gave me great faith to believe in the impossible.

I have since learned you cannot base your life on those of others. We all must work out our salvation with fear and trembling. I had many detours in life like Joseph along the way. My brothers and sisters rejected me because of my imagination or dreams and faith to believe in God at all costs. I was stripped of things like relationships because of other people's opinions. However, it allowed me to discover that Christ is a friend that sticks closer than any brother. I was lied on by some of my closest confidants. Many promises were made to me as I would give people a word from the Lord that came to pass. In return, just as the butler and the baker did Joseph when they arrived at their wealthy place, they forgot all about me. However, these trials burned away my limitation to believe in God over man. I have lived my life based on this scripture *(Isaiah 54:17). NIV* *"No weapon forged against you will prevail, and you will refute every tongue that accuses you. This is the heritage of the servants of the LORD, and this is their vindication from me," declares the LORD."*

The trials of this magnitude burned away my limitations and taught me how powerful my Savior is. The fire of abandonment, broken marriages, financial devastation, sickness, and rejection burned away all my doubts God is all that He says He is. My trials became my steppingstones to greatness. I learned to kiss the hammer and chisel the Lord uses to make me a ready vessel. The diamond in the rough was the journey I had to take. It was in those dark places I saw the light of Christ shining in my life. My faith was tried in many areas. In my opinion, I had to forgive the unforgivable or those that I thought were unforgivable. However, God taught me he forgives the vilest of sinners. It was not my place to judge a man's sin but love them as he loved me. The only individual he would not forgive is one who blasphemes the Holy Spirit. In some of those most painful trials, I learned the power of forgiveness.

Those trials burned away my limitation of mans' way of loving. The Fire of the Holy Spirit taught me how to love those who had betrayed me. Once I surmounted the pain of being betrayed, I soared like an eagle to a new height in Christ. I bore the mark of my Heavenly Father in my body. Indeed, my trials made me strong. It produced a humility that I could not explain. I learned that where I was limited, my God was limitless. I had to trust the process and because I gave my complete yes to the Lord, the sky was the limit. Instead of the fires of my life destroying me. It redefined me and realigned me into a beautiful vessel God could use for His Glory.

Food for thought:

Trials and Tribulations are used to develop us and rid us of doubt.

What fire has tried to destroy you?

Let the fire of Gods' Word burn your limitations.

CHAPTER 11
THE FATHER'S LOVE

The father's love is so needed and necessary today. A father figure is so important in the lives of their children. Without it, the DNA is incomplete, and they do not know who they are. I learned this firsthand from my own personal experience of having my father alienated from my life for the first seven years. We know earthly fathers are needed so is our heavenly father, for he created us when we were yet in our mother's womb. He is the author and the finisher of our faith. He knows our life from the beginning to the end. The father is the one that validates us.

Once I discovered who my earthly father was, I was made whole and complete. My earthly father introduced me to my heavenly Father. I highly respected him for that because when he couldn't fulfill his obligation, although he tried, my Heavenly Father fulfilled those voids in my life.

Dr. Melinda Watts

John 3:16 KJV "God so loved the world that he gave his only begotten son…".

Once I realized the power of his love, my life changed for the better. My earthly father taught me how to live but the greatest legacy he left me was my Lord and Savior, Jesus Christ. My Heavenly Father taught me how to live without my earthly father. My earthly father was my everything. I knew he loved unconditionally. He made me feel special, loved, and beautiful. However, my Heavenly Father loves me more than my earthly father. He loved me through that difficult moment of my father transitioning to Glory. My earthly father's love demonstrated my heavenly Father's love. They knew me better than I knew myself. The love of my father caused him to pray for me daily. I know it was his prayers that kept me all those years. Now, God the Father, Son, and God the Holy Spirit prays for me. He makes intercession for me daily. He loves me unconditionally. My life was like the woman at the well.

I needed a savior to quench my thirst for love, acceptance, and satisfaction. His love for me looked beyond my faults and saws my needs. His love is so amazing. His love keeps me focused. I never knew love like this before. His love corrects me when I am wrong. His love comforts me in areas I am deficient. His love sustains me and keeps me from harm's way. I am who I am because of his love. His love covered me in my iniquities. His love is patient with me when I am impatient with myself. His loves teach me, like a child, to always have faith in him. I have seen His love in so many ways. His love is very dependable. He is my daddy, Abba Father; I can cry out to him, and he answers me. His love leads me on the path of righteousness. His love resolves all my insecurities. His love is necessary for me to thrive. His love is his word, and it daily fills my hunger to know more about him. His love keeps me chasing after him like the deer that pants after the water. My soul pants after more of his love. His love wakes me up in the morning and his love watches over me while I sleep. His love makes melodies in my heart. His love gives me new songs to sing. His love protects me from my adversaries. His love is indescribable, uncontainable, and unlimited. My Father's love has no hidden agenda. His love for me is reckless.

When I am weary and worn, I run into his presence and his love restores me. My Father's Love keeps me when I don't want to be kept. His Love gently caresses my heart when it becomes anxious. If I had thousands of tongues, it could not express my Father's Love for me. His love caused him to die for me. What a sacrifice. His Love suffered for me. His love captured me. His love spared me. His love gave me access to his throne. His love revealed who I am to me. His love said I was the apple of his eye. His love said I was fearful and wondrously made. His love said I was more than a conqueror. His love imparted his DNA into me. His love taught me how to forgive. His love taught me how to give. My Father's love can never be replaced. His love is his amazing grace. His love healed all my hurts and diseases. His love taught me that Jesus is real. His love taught me the importance of kneeling. His love taught me never to quit. His love never failed me. His love delivered me. His love is unquenchable. His love showed me that which was meant to destroy me redefined me. His love said to the fire, you can't burn her; she is mine. His love used the fire to realign me.

Dr. Melinda Watts

Food for thought

God so loved the world that he gave his only begotten son. (St. John 3:16)KJV

Ask the Lord to let you experience his genuine love if you need love.

I want to encourage the readers of this book to never allow your beginning to determine your ending. Press toward the mark of the higher calling which is in Christ Jesus. His desire is to change your story. The prayer of Jabez is a powerful prayer. Jabez was born in pain and sorrow. His name meant sorrow. It was his prayer life that changed his course in life. He prayed for the Lord to bless him, enlarge his territory, keep his hands on him, keep him from harm so he would be free from pain. We all have experience some type of pain in our lives yet when we cast all of our cares upon the lord, he will heal us from all of our infirmities. Do not allow the negative start in life determine who you are. We are fearfully and wondrously made. Just like the woman who had the issue of blood for twelve long years, however when she touched the hem of his garment she was made whole. His consuming fire of the word healed her. The same consuming fire will heal us if we continue to surrender our will to his perfect will. May the Lord richly bless you and keep you. Never stop believing and just like me that which was meant to destroy is now your testimony to heal others.

ABOUT THE AUTHOR

Dr. Melinda W. Watts is the daughter of Addie Mae Walker and Avery Bryant. A native of Washington DC. Her walk with the Lord started on September 22, 1989. Her gift of singing, teaching, preaching, and prophesying has set her before great men and women. Dr. Watts is using her gifts to advance the kingdom of God immensely. She accredits all the Glory to God.

Dr. Watts holds a Doctorate Degree in Theology from the School of the Great Commission. She is the Campus

Dean of IIWC School of the Great Commission in Columbia, Maryland and Wahiawa, Hawaii. She is the Founder of the following ministries: Integrity International Worship Center Batesburg SC and Integrity International Center Wahiawa Hawaii. In addition, she has a nonprofit organization for women and children called Hagar's Restoration Home. It offers Hope, acceptance, grace, assurance, and restoration.

She has founded several outreach ministries such as Single Yet Unique, Cup of Coffee with Jesus Podcast and Beyond Walls Outreach. Dr. Watt is an anointed psalmist who has recorded several musical projects such as Be Still, Faithful, and a single written by her daughter Phaedra Jones entitled You Alone. Her Motto is I can do all things through Christ who strengthens me.

Dr. Watts is the wife of Minister Ronald Watts. They have a family of nine children and eight grandchildren. They reside In Columbia, Maryland.

She has now accepted the mandate to reach the masses locally, nationally, and internationally.

Thanks so much for purchasing this book. Proceeds go to help women in crisis.

If you would like more information about Hagar's Restoration House, in need of a Preacher, Psalmist or motivational speaker please feel free to contact me: Hagarshome52@gmail.com

SITED

King James Version, Thomasnelsonbibles.com, Biblehub.com

New International Version Holy Bible, New International Version NIV, Copyright 1973, 1978, 1984, 2011 by Biblica Inc, Biblegateway.com

Printed in the United States
by Baker & Taylor Publisher Services